Is It Saturday Yet?

Joke and Riddle Book

Illustrations by J. Corbitt
Cover Photo by Robert Cushman Hayes

Antioch Publishing Company
Yellow Springs, Ohio 45387

Copyright © 1983 by Antioch Publishing Company
Made in the United States of America

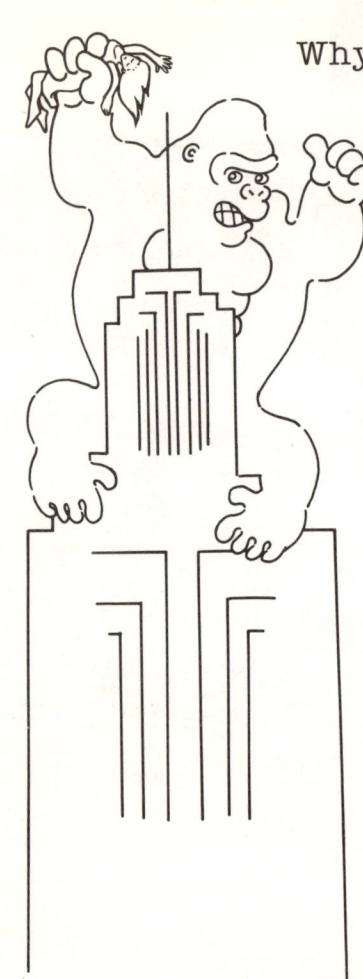

Why did the giant ape climb up the side of the Empire State Building?
🐾 The elevator was broken.

Which American President did apes like best?
🐾 Ape Lincoln

Where was the gorilla when the lights went out?
🐾 In the dark

What do you get when you cross a gorilla with a parrot?
🐾 I don't know, but when it talks, you'd better listen.

Where do you look for a gorilla?
🐾 Wherever you left him

What should you do if you find a gorilla asleep in your bed?
🐾 Sleep somewhere else

If a skunk had a stuffy nose, how would it smell?
🐾 As bad as ever

Should we get fur from a skunk?
🐾 Yes—as fur as possible

What did the judge say when the skunk walked into the courtroom?
🐾 "Odor in the court."

What do you get if you cross an owl with a skunk?
🐾 A bird that smells bad but doesn't give a hoot

Why is a skunk like a chauffeur?
🐾 They both drive you away.

Why shouldn't you grab a lion by his tail?
🐾 It may only be his tail, but it could be your end.

What happened when the lion swallowed a flashlight?
🐾 He hiccuped with delight.

Why did the lion cub sleep with the fan on?
🐾 She wanted to be a cool cat.

What did Tarzan say when he saw the lions coming toward him?
🐾 "Here come the lions."

Name ten African animals in three seconds?
🐾 Nine lions . . .
and a giraffe

What was the king of the jungle called?
🐾 The emper-ROAR

Cool cat!

What animal always sleeps with its shoes on?

🐾 A horse

How can you read while riding a horse at night?

🐾 Use a saddle-light (satelite).

How do you get down from a horse?

🐾 You don't. You get down from a duck.

Why is a horseback rider like a cloud?

🐾 They both hold reins (rains).

What kind of dreams do horses have?

🐾 Nightmares

Teddy: I went riding this morning.
Betty: Horseback?
Teddy: Oh, yes. She got back 2 hours before I did.

How do you catch a rabbit?
🐾 Hide in the bushes and make a noise like a carrot.

What is the difference between a crazy rabbit and a counterfeit quarter?
🐾 One is a mad bunny, and the other is bad money.

How can you spell rabbit without using the letter "R"?
🐾 B-U-N-N-Y

What do you get when you cross an insect with a rabbit?
🐾 Bugs Bunny

Why did Silly Billy wash his rabbit?
🐾 Because someone said his hare was dirty

How do rabbits travel?
🐾 By hareplane (airplane)

What does an electric rabbit say?
🐾 "Watts up, Doc?"

What did the raccoon say after it flew from California to New York?
🐾 "Boy! My arms are tired."

When is a raccoon not a raccoon?
🐾 When it eats too much and makes a pig of itself

Why do raccoons like to go out to eat with leopards?
🐾 Because leopards know all the good spots

What's the best way to catch a raccoon?
🐾 Have someone throw it to you.

Can a raccoon jump higher than a house?
🐾 Of course—houses can't jump.

Did you hear about the man who went horseback riding in the woods? He was surprised when a raccoon said, "Good morning!"

"I didn't know raccoons could talk," said the man.

"Neither did I," said his horse.

How do you make an elephant float?
🐾 Two scoops of ice cream, some root beer, and an elephant

How do you know there's an elephant in the refrigerator?
🐾 The door won't shut.

What would you get if you crossed an elephant with a mouse?
🐾 Huge holes in the wall

What's the difference between a chicken and an elephant?
🐾 About a ton

Why do elephants paint their toenails red?
🐾 So they can hide in a strawberry patch

Why are elephants large, gray, and wrinkled?
🐾 Because if they were small, round, and white, they would be aspirin

If a chicken crosses the road, rolls in the mud, then crosses back again, what is it?
🐾 A dirty double-crosser

What do you get when you cross a duck with a cow?
🐾 Milk and quackers (crackers)

Why did the farmer scold the chickens?
🐾 Because they used "fowl" language

Who's never hungry on Thanksgiving?
🐾 The turkey—it's stuffed

Why is a coin like a bird sitting on a branch?
🐾 Both have heads on one side, tails on the other.

What do ducks do when they fly upside down?
🐾 They quack up.

What did the bear do when it hurt its foot?
🐾 It called a toe truck (tow truck).

Why does a bear sleep through the winter?
🐾 Would you dare wake up a sleeping bear?

How do you get fur from a bear?
🐾 Run fast in the opposite direction!

What do bears have that no other animal has?
🐾 Bear cubs

What animal do you look like when you take a bath?
🐾 A little bear (bare)

Where does a polar bear keep money?
🐾 In a snow bank

What has 8 legs and is sticky?
🐾 Two bears eating honey

What does a cat read every morning?
🐾 The MEWS-paper

Why is Christmas Eve like a cat jogging along the beach?
🐾 They both have sandy claws (Santa Claus).

How did the cat behave when it met the queen?
🐾 PURR-fectly

What do people from Australia call baby Siamese cats?
🐾 Kittens

How did the cat feel after it was hit by a bus?
🐾 It had that rundown feeling.

What kind of cat never says meow?
🐾 A catfish

What do you call a chimpanzee that sticks its right paw down a lion's throat?
🐾 Lefty

Why do chimps like bananas?
🐾 Because they have a peel (appeal)

What kind of cookies do monkeys eat?
🐾 Chocolate chimp cookies

How many monkeys will fit in an empty room?
🐾 One—after that the room isn't empty

What monkey is a winner?
🐾 A chimp-ion

When does a chimp chase a banana?
🐾 When the banana splits